GW00455743

WELCOME TO THE PLATINUM JUBILEE QUIZ BOOK

Paragon Publishing offers a wide selection of other quiz and crossword books, so be sure to check them out if you enjoy this one.

Paragon Publishing is a privately run publishing company which cares greatly about the accuracy of its content.

As many facts and figures in this book are subject to change, please email us at **ParagonPublishing23@gmail.com** if you notice any inaccuracies to help us keep our book as up-to-date and as accurate as possible.

If you have enjoyed this book please leave us a review on Amazon.

Have fun!

CONTENTS

Early life   4

Other royalty   8

Jubilee history   11

Milestones and annual events   14

Coronation   17

Jubilee 2022   20

Royal properties   23

Miscellaneous   26

Match the title to the name   33

Line of succession   34

Answers

Early life   37

Other royalty   38

Jubilee history   39

Milestones and annual events   40

Coronation   41

Jubilee 2022   42

Royal properties   43

Miscellaneous   44

Match the title to the name   46

Line of succession   47

Early Life

1. Which month was Queen Elizabeth born in?

2. Which month is her official birthday?

3. Which year was she born in?
a. 1924   b. 1925   c. 1926   d. 1927

4. What is her full name?

5. Her birthplace is now a restaurant of which cuisine?
a. Italian   b. Mexican   c. Thai   d. Cantonese

6. What is the name of the first corgi she ever owned?
a. Susan   b. Mary   c. Caroline   d. Dorothy

7. What is the name of her first pony, a Shetland she received at 4 years old from her grandfather, King George V?
a. Zippy   b. Charlotte   c. Peggy   d. Sugar

8. What is the name of the Queen's father?

9. The Queen's father was the Duke of where?

10. What was Elizabeth's nickname as a child?

11. A young Princess Elizabeth had a doll in a red coat with a matching beret (which remains in the Royal Collection today). What is her name?
a. Agnes   b. Pamela   c. Beatrice   d. Harriet

12. What did a young Elizabeth call her grandfather, King George V?

13. During her grandfather's reign, where was Elizabeth in the line of succession?
a. First   b. Second   c. Third   d. Fourth

14. In 1945, what did a young Elizabeth train as with the Auxiliary Territorial Service?
a. Nurse   b. Midwife   c. Ambulance driver

15. On which day did a young Elizabeth and Margaret escape Buckingham Palace to celebrate in the streets?

16. Where was she when she celebrated her 21st birthday?
a. South Africa   b. Portugal   c. Spain   d. Jamaica

17. Elizabeth was in this African country when she discovered that she was Queen.
a. Egypt   b. Uganda   c. Kenya   d. Ghana

18. Name the location where Elizabeth and Philip met for the second time, and decided to start courting.

19. How old was Elizabeth when their engagement was officially announced?
a. 18   b. 19   c. 20   d. 21

20. Where did they marry?

21. The Queen shares a birthday with Charlotte Brontë, James McAvoy and which other famous pop star?
a. Iggy Pop   b. Michael Jackson
c. Jennifer Lopez   d. Beyonce

22. Marion Crawford, who was known to the young Queen as 'Crawfie', was later ostracised by the Royal family. Why?
a. She went to work for the President of America
b. She had an illegitimate child
c. She sold her story to the press
d. She married a divorcee

23. Starting in 1938, Princess Elizabeth was tutored by Henry Marten in constitutional history. What was his day job?
a. Vice-provost of Eton College
b. Admiral in the Royal Navy
c. Sergeant in the army
d. Lecturer at Oxford University

24. Where did Princess Elizabeth first meet Prince Philip in 1934?

a. At a lunch in Balmoral Castle
b. Aboard the Royal Yacht
c. At the wedding of mutual relatives
d. By chance at a tennis club

OTHER ROYALTY

1. What is the maiden surname of the Queen's mother?

2. Which member of the royal family once competed in the 1976 Olympics?

3. Which member of the royal family competed in the 2012 Olympics?

4. What is the relation of these two Olympians?

5. In which sport did they both compete in?

6. At which university did Will and Kate meet?
a. Oxford b. Cambridge c. Manchester d. St Andrews

7. Which subject did they both major in?

8. Which royal graduated from Newcastle University?
a. Princess Beatrice b. Princess Louise
c. Princess Eugenie d. Prince Henry

9. Who was the first member of the royal family to be born in Scotland for more than 300 years?
a. Princess Alexandra b. Princess Margaret
c. Prince Michael d. Prince Richard

10. Who is the current Duke of Cornwall?

11. In which Commonwealth country did Prince Charles spend two terms as a schoolboy in 1966?
a. India   b. Canada   c. New Zealand   d. Australia

12. Which royal spent some of their gap year in Lesotho?

13. Which princess was formerly a teacher?
a. Princess Anne   b. Princess Diana   c. Princess Caroline

14. Who is the current Earl of Wessex?

15. Which royal married an Italian noble in 2020?

16. Which royal briefly lived in Jordan during their childhood?

17. Where did Harry trek to in 2011 to raise awareness for wounded servicemen and women?
a. Everest base camp   b. From France to Afghanistan
c. The North Pole   d. The Sahara Desert

18. Which royal was nicknamed 'Billy the Fish' during their military service?
a. Prince William   b. Prince Charles   c. Prince Harry

19. What is the name of the divorcee who King Edward VIII abdicated the throne in order to marry?

20. In which year did Anne, the Princess Royal, survive a kidnapping attempt?

a. 1966   b. 1968   c. 1970   d. 1972

JUBILEE HISTORY

1. Although Edward III did not officially celebrate his Golden Jubilee in 1377, he did host a spectacular week long event. What was it?

a. Fine arts commpetition

b. Horse racing

c. A week of no work for the whole country

d. Jousting

2. Who is credited with being the first monarch to mark a Golden Jubilee?

3. In which year did George III celebrate his Golden Jubilee?

a. 1799 b. 1804 c. 1809 d. 1814

4. What was different about when George III celebrated his Golden Jubilee?

a. It was his 51st year of being King

b. It was celebrated at the start of the year

c. He did not attend the celebrations

d. King George became drunk for the first time since being King

5. When did Queen Victoria celebrate her Golden Jubilee?

a. 1887 b. 1889 c. 1891 d. 1893

6. How many foreign Kings and Princes attended Queen Victoria's Golden Jubilee feast?
a. 10   b. 25   c. 50   d. 100

7. List the names of the following Jubilee's:
25th anniversary:
40th anniversary:
50th anniversary:
60th anniversary:
65th anniversary:
70th anniversary:

8. At which Cathedral did Queen Victoria celebrate her Diamond Jubilee?

9. Which Jubilee did King George V celebrate on 6 May 1935?

10. When did Queen Elizabeth celebrate her Silver Jubilee?
a. 1975   b. 1976   c. 1977   d. 1978

11. How many people watched Queen Elizabeth's Silver Jubilee?
a. 200 million   b. 300 million
c. 400 million   d. 500 million

12. When was Queen Elizabeth's Golden Jubilee?

13. In which year did Queen Elizabeth overtake Queen Victoria to become the longest-living British monarch?
a. 2004   b. 2005   c. 2006   d. 2007

14. One of the highlights of Queen Elizabeth's Diamond Jubilee was the Thames River Pagent. During this, 1000 boats travelled from Chelsea to where?

15. Which popular song did Brian May play at the Golden Jubilee "Party at the Palace"?
a. Dancing Queen   b. Killer Queen
c. God Save the Queen

MILESTONES AND ANNUAL EVENTS

1. How many Roman Catholic Popes have there been during her reign?
a. 5   b. 6   c. 7   d. 8

2. Name the annual party which the Queen hosts to support disabled veterans.

3. Name the ceremony which celebrates the Queen's official birthday.

4. Name the annual ceremony which is concerned with the conservation of Swans along the River Thames.

5. Queen Elizabeth was the first British Monarch to ever visit which country in 1986?
a. Japan   b. China   c. Brazil   d. Thailand

6. What is the name of Buckingham Palace's first women-only event in March 2004?

7. She was the first monarch to open Parliament in this country. Which country is this?

8. In which year did the Queen first visit West Germany, signalling the reconciliation between the countries.
a. 1964   b. 1965   c. 1966   d. 1967

9. The Queen's first state visit as monarch was to which country in 1953?
a. Costa Rica   b. Guatemala   c. Belize   d. Panama

10. Although she never went to school, the Queen did earn professional qualifications in this sector.
a. Nursing   b. Teaching   c. Driving   d. Horse-riding

11. Which year does the Queen describe as her 'annus horribilis'?
a. 1988   b. 1990   c. 1992   d. 1994

12. Which events occurred in the year of 'annus horribilis'?

13. The British edition of which famous fashion magazine featured the Queen on its cover for the first time this April?
a. Marie Claire   b. Elle   c. Vogue   d. Harper's Bizaar

14. After touring this country in October 1972, Elizabeth became the first British monarch to visit which communist country?

15. What colour was the neon suit she wore for her 90th birthday celebration?

16. Elizabeth's visit to which country in 2011 was historic because it was the first visit by a British monarch since its independence?

17. On a particular Thursday, the Queen distributes which type of coin to senior citizens?

18. Which horticultural show is often attended by the Queen and other Royals every May?

19. In which month is Commonwealth Day?
a. March   b. April   c. May   d. June

20. Currently, how many generations of direct heirs to the British throne are alive at the same time?
a. Two   b. Three   c. Four   d. Five

CORONATION

1. When did the Coronation occur?
a. 1950   b. 1951   c. 1952   d. 1953

2. Where was the Coronation held?

3. For which reason was the coronation of Queen Elizabeth II was groundbreaking?
a. It was the first coronation on a Sunday
b. It was the first coronation on the monarch's birthday
c. It was the first to be televised
d. It was the longest coronation in history

4. How many Queens had been coronated in their own right before Queen Elizabeth II?
a. 4   b. 5   c. 6   d. 7

5. How many guests attended the Coronation ceremony?
a. 8251   b. 11045   c. 16395   d. 24008

6. Who was the designer of the Queen's Coronation dress?
a. Matthew Williamson   b. Norman Hartnell
c. Stephen Jones   d. Catherine Rayner

7. The royal designer of the Coronation dress included emblems from many Commonwealth countries, such as the shamrock for Northern Ireland and the maple leaf for Canada. What was the emblem for India?

8. What was the emblem for Wales?
a. Potato   b. Cabbage   c. Leek   d. Beetroot

9. What is the name of the globular royal item which the queen carried in her right hand during the coronation ceremony?

10. What does this represent?

11. Which diamond is embedded in the Sceptre used during the Queen's Coronation?

12. What colour was the Queen's dress during the most sacred part of the Coronation - the anointing?
a. Blue   b. Red   c. Black   d. White

13. Which two flowers made up the bulk of the Queen's bouquet?
a. Poppies   b. Roses   c. Lillies   d. Orchids   e. Daffodils

14. One of the swords used in the Queen's Coronation has a broken tip, which is meant to represent which virtue?
a. Honesty   b. Courage   c. Generosity   d. Mercy

15. The Coronation service is divided into six parts. In which part is the crowning?
a. The investiture   b. The anointing
c. The enthronement   d. The oath

16. In the Coronation service, what was described as 'the most valuable thing'?

17. What is the name of the crown which the Queen wore during her coronation?

18. What is the name of the crown Queen Elizabeth wore after her Coronation, as she stood on the balcony of Buckingham Palace and waved to the crowds?

19. This popular sandwich filling was invented for the foreign guests of the Coronation.

20. The Coronation ring is also known as what?

21. During the coronation, the monarch is anointed with oils containing roses, cinnamon, orange, musk and what else?
a. Cat hair   b. Elephant semen   c. Whale poo

JUBILEE 2022

1. What is the name of the competition which searches nationwide for the perfect dessert to celebrate this historic event?

2. Which colour was the National Carillon lit up to honour the start of the Platinum Jubilee year?
a. Red   b. Purple   c. Green   d. White

3. Which day marked the start of the Platinum Jubilee celebrations?

4. How did the Queen sign her 2022 speech?

5. The Queen's Baton will feature a platinum strand this year for which event?

6. New Zealand celebrates the Jubilee year by investing in which environmentally sustainable programme?
a. Beach cleaning   b. Subsidised solar panels
c. Tree planting   d. Reduction of oil usage

7. What is the name of the font used in the Platinum Jubilee emblem, which means 'forever'?
a. Eternitea   b. Infinitea   c. Eonua   d. Perpetua

8. Where will the Queen attend the Derby on the 4th of June?

9. Communities are encouraged to have a ___ _____ _____ on the 5th of June. Fill in the blank.

10. What is the name of the national day of gratitude that will be held on the 5th of June to commemorate the Queen's Platinum Jubilee?

11. What is the name of an exhibition at a royal Scottish Castle, which will run for several months in celebration of the Jubilee Year?

12. What is the name of the flower display at the moat of the Tower of London?
a. Royal bloom   b. Her Majesty's bloom
c. Superbloom   d. Everlong bloom

13. Which condiment company released limited-edition bottles to celebrate the Platinum Jubilee?

14. Two of the following are these special-edition condiments. Can you guess which ones they are?
a. Salad Queen   b. HM Sauce   c. Majesty Mayo
d. Jubilee Jam   e. Kingdom Ketchup

15. Which days in June will the Jubilee be taking place?

16. Approximately how many horses will there be at her birthday celebration?
a. 100   b. 180   c. 240   d. 320

17. How many beacons will be lit at the Queen's birthday celebrations?
a. Over 700   b. Over 1100   c. Over 1500   d. Over 1900

18. The church bell at St Paul's Cathedral will ring for the first time for a royal occaision since it was restored. How many times has it rung since it was restored?
a. 1   b. 8   c. 32   d. 105

19. True or false: there will still be the same number of Bank Holidays in Britain this year despite the four-day bank holiday.

20. The Royal Mint and the Royal Canadian Mint have partnered to create a two coin-set for the Jubilee. What are the two images of the Queen that appear on these coins?
a. Equestrian portrait of the Queen
b. Portrait of the Queen playing croquet
c. Portrait of the Queen at her Golden Jubilee
d. Portrait of the Queen in 1952

ROYAL PROPERTIES

1. What is the oldest occupied castle in the world, and where the Queen spends many private weekends?

2. What is the name of the Queen's private Scottish estate, where she spends her summers?

3. What is the Queen's private country home in Norfolk called, where the Royal Family spends Christmas?

4. Name the principal royal residence in Scotland, based in Edinburgh, where she spends one week at the end of June each year.

5. What is the name of the Queen's official residence in Northern Ireland?

6. How many acres does Windsor Castle occupy?
a. 10   b. 13   c. 16   d. 19

7. The Royal Estate at Windsor accommodates around 1500 Lohmann Browns. What are they?

8. What is the name of the Commonwealth country that the Queen lived in for a short time when she was a young woman?

9. What is the name of Prince Charles' official residence?

10. The people of Wales gifted the queen a property called 'Y Bwthyn Bach', which translates to what in English?
a. Royal house   b. Cosy cottage
c. Little cottage   d. Royal den

11. Name the Royal property found on the Isles of Scilly.

12. What is the name of Princess Eugenie's residence in Berkshire?
a. Livergate Cottage   b. Frogmore Cottage
c. Butterfly Cottage   d. Chihuahua Cottage

13. Y Bwthyn Bach was the first property which the Queen owned. How old was she when it was gifted to her?
a. 4   b. 6   c. 8   d. 10

14. For which exotic crop has an acre of ground been set aside at Sandringham?
a. Hemp   b. Black truffles
c. Cherry tomato   d. Zucchini

15. For many years the house at Sandringham was ahead of the Greenwich Mean Time. How much time ahead were they?
a. 30 minutes   b. 1 hour   c. 90 minutes   d. 2 hours

16. At which of the following of the Queens properties can you go on a safari?
a. Holyroodhouse   b. Balmoral Estate
c. Windosor Great Park

17. St George's Chapel at Windsor Castle is known as a Royal Peculiar. What is the meaning of this?

18. Which tiny royal residence can be found within Windsor Castle, which itself has many small items of value?
a. The Duke of Cornwall's garden shed
b. Prince Charles' tree house
c. Queen Mary's dolls' house

19. Which royal property was offered by William IV as an alternative place for Parliament when it was destroyed by a fire in 1834?

MISCELLANEOUS

1. How many Prime Ministers has the Queen been served by?
a. 10   b. 12   c. 14   d. 16

2. Which PM served her for the longest?

3. Name the breed of dog that the Queen is credited with creating?

4. Which football team does she support?
a. Tottenham   b. West Ham
c. Crystal Palace   d. Arsenal

5. She is the face of which down under currency?

6. Which other language does she speak fluently?
a. German   b. Spanish   c. French   d. Welsh

7. What is the name of her last corgi, who died in 2018?
a. Whisper   b. Genie   c. Puppet   d. Snuffles

8. Which unusual animal does she like to race?

9. She used the London Tube for the second time in 1969 for the opening of which Line?

10. Which strange gift did she recieve from the government of the Australian state of Queensland, because food rationing was still in effect?

11. What breed were the Queen's dogs: Bisto, Oxo, Flash, Spick and Span?

12. The Queen's dogs appeared in which blockbuster film series?
a. Harry Potter   b. James Bond
c. Jason Bourne   d. Mission Impossible

13. Which country gifted the Queen with sloths in 1968?
a. Brazil   b. Mexico   c. South Africa   d. Peru

14. Who was first PM to be born in the Queen's reign?
a. Margaret Thatcher   b. John Major
c. Tony Blair   d. Gordon Brown

15. Which Harry Potter house did the Queen name one of her dogs after?
a. Hufflepuff   b. Gryffindor
c. Ravenclaw   d. Slytherin

16. What is the accessory that the queen wears to honour her late father?

17. Which item of clothing broke on Elizabeth and Philip's wedding day in 1947?
a. Her dress   b. Necklace   c. Shoe   d. Tiara

18. Which instrument is used to wake the Queen up every morning?
a. Harp   b. Flute   c. Bagpipes   d. Accordion

19. What is her official Bard called?

20. Which baby animal was born at Cotswold Wildlife Park in April 2022 and was christened 'Queenie'?
a. Elephant   b. Tiger   c. Rhino   d. Grizzly Bear

21. What was the Queen's wedding dress bought with?
a. Pennies   b. Ration coupons   c. Its own weight in gold

22. Who is the only President of the United States that the Queen did not meet during her reign?

23. Who did Princess Margaret call off her engagement to in 1955?

24. Which of the following fish is automatically property of the Queen if caught in the UK?
a. Carp   b. Sturgeon   c. Salmon   d. Mackerel

25. Which of the following animals is bred at Hampton Court?
a. Cows   b. Fell ponies   c. Goats   d. Alpacas

26. None of the Queens horses have ever won a celebrated race. Aureole's second place finish in her coronation year came at which race?
a. The Grand National   b. The Cheltenham Gold Cup
c. The Derby

27. What was the name of the first Corgi that the Queen was given on her 18th birthday?
a. Sarah   b. Penelope   c. Susan   d. Rachel

28. What role did Anthony Blunt play in the Household before he was unmasked as a Russian spy?
a. Surveyor of the Queen's Pictures
b. Keeper of the Royal Secrets
c. Somerset King of Arms

29. Name the noisy job that William Ross fulfilled for 37 years for the royal family.
a. Bird-scarer at Balmoral Castle
b. Private singer to the Queen
c. Piper to the Sovereign

30. Which main dish was served at the wedding breakfast of the Queen and the Duke of Edinburgh in 1947?

a. Haggis   b. Chicken curry
c. Coq au vin   d. Partridge casserole

31. Which of the following foods does the Queen not like?

a. Prawns   b. Squid   c. Lobster   d. Oysters

32. Which of the following would it also be ill advised to serve to the Queen as she dislikes it?

a. Ginger   b. Rosemary   c. Chilli   d. Garlic

33. The Queen is very fond of a Scottish dish called Gleneagles pâté. What are the main ingredients of this dish?

a. Chicken livers

b. Smoked salmon, trout and mackerel

c. Crab stick and parsely

34. Which of the following cereals is the Queen fond of at breakfast time?

a. Frosties   b. Rice Krispies   c. Special K   d. Porridge

35. All menus at the Queens banquets are written in which language?

a. French   b. Latin   c. Spanish   d. Gaelic

36. Which nationality is the current Royal Train operator DB from?

37. There are 54 members of the Commonwealth. The Queen has visited all but two. Which two has she not visited?
a. Malaysia   b. Malawi   c. Cameroon
d. Rwanda   e. Kenya   d. Papua New Guinea

38. What was strange about when the Queen visited the US in 1957 and 1959?
a. Didn't meet the President either time
b. It was only for refuelling
c. She was visiting in her role as Queen of Canada

39. Where was the Queens second international visit as Queen in 1954 to, where she was hosted by King Idris?
a. Swaziland   b. Rwanda   c. Libya   d. Namibia

40. When on tour, the Queen is always accompanied by her own supply of transfusible blood, bottled water and what else?
a. Tea   b. Coffee   c. Fudge   d. Toilet paper

41. Which King had the idea that monarchs should be able to celebrate a second official birthday?
a. Henry VIII   b. Charles II   c. Henry II   d. George II

42. Each royal wedding from 1840 to 2011 has included what?
a. Confetti   b. Tea and scones   c. Fruitcake

43. Whilst celebrating her Diamond Jubilee, the Queen gave city status to which British city?

44. On which social media did the Queen post on for the first time ever on March 7, 2019?
a. Instagram   b. Facebook   c. Twitter   d. Tiktok

MATCH THE TITLE TO THE NAME

1. Prince of Wales

2. Duke and Duchess of Cambridge

3. Earl of Wessex

4. Duke of Gloucester

5. Duke of Kent

6. Duke of York

7. Duke of Edinburgh

8. Duke of Cornwall

9. Earl of Snowdon

10. Duchess of Windsor

LINE OF SUCCESSION

This round will give you 20 people in line to become King or Queen, with some letters given to help. More letters will be given as the names become more obscure.

1st _ _ _ _ _ _   _ _ _ _ _ _ _

2nd _ _ _ _ _ _   _ _ _ _ _ _ _

3rd _ _ _ _ _ _   _ _ _ _ _ _

4th _ _ _ _ _ _ _ _   _ _ _ _ _ _ _ _ _

5th _ _ _ _ _ _   _ _ _ _ _

6th _ _ _ _ _ _   _ _ _ _ _

7th _ _ c _ _   _ _ _ n _ _ a _ _ _ _ - _ _ _ _ _ r

8th _ _ _ _ b _ _   D _ _ _ _   _ _ _ _ t _ _ _ _ e _   _ _ _ d _ _ _

9th _ _ _ _ _ _   _ n _ _ _ w

10th P_____e__ __at____

11th ____ce__ _u___i_

12th A___s_ ___li_ _aw__ __oo____n_

13th ____ce __w__d

14th __m__, V____u_t ___er_

15th ___y _ou___ __nd___

16th A__e __in____ R___l

17th _et__ _h__l___

18th S___nn__ __ill___

19th _sl_ P____ip_

20th Z___ T_____l

ANSWERS

EARLY LIFE

1. April
2. June
3. 1926
4. Elizabeth Alexandra Mary Windsor
5. Cantonese
6. Susan
7. Peggy
8. Albert
9. York
10. Lilibet
11. Pamela
12. Grandpa England
13. Third
14. Ambulance driver
15. VE Day 1945
16. South Africa
17. Kenya
18. Royal Naval College in Dartmouth
19. 21
20. Westminster Abbey
21. Iggy Pop
22. She sold her story to the press
23. Vice-provost of Eton College
24. At the wedding of mutual relatives

OTHER ROYALTY

1. Bowes-Lyon
2. Princess Anne
3. Zara Tindall
4. Mother and daughter
5. Equestrian
6. St Andrews
7. History of art
8. Princess Eugenie
9. Princess Margaret
10. Prince Charles
11. Australia
12. Harry
13. Princess Diana
14. Prince Edward
15. Princess Beatrice
16. Kate Middleton
17. The North Pole
18. Prince William
19. Wallis Simpson
20. 1972

JUBILEE HISTORY

1. Jousting

2. George III

3. 1809

4. It was celebrated at the start of the year

5. 1887

6. 50

7. 25th anniversary - Silver

40th anniversary - Ruby

50th anniversary - Gold

60th anniversary - Diamond

65th anniversary - Sapphire

70th anniversary - Platinum

8. St. Paul's Cathedral

9. Silver

10. 1977

11. 500 million

12. 2002

13. 2007

14. Tower Bridge

15. God Save the Queen

MILESTONES AND ANNUAL EVENTS

1. Six
2. Not Forgotten Garden Party
3. Trooping the Colour
4. Swan Upping
5. China
6. Women of Achievement
7. Canada
8. 1965
9. Panama
10. Driving
11. 1992
12. Fire at Windsor castle and the divorces of three of her children
13. Vogue
14. Yugoslavia
15. Lime Green
16. Ireland
17. Royal Maundy
18. Chelsea Flower Show
19. March
20. Three

CORONATION

1. 1953
2. Westminster Abbey
3. The first to be televised
4. 5
5. 8251
6. Norman Hartnell
7. Lotus Flower
8. Leek
9. The Sovereign Orb
10. The Christian World
11. The Cullinan Diamond
12. White
13. Orchids and Lillies
14. Mercy
15. The investiture
16. The Bible
17. St Edward's Crown
18. The Imperial State Crown
19. Coronation chicken
20. The Wedding Ring of England
21. Whale poo

Jubilee 2022

1. The Platinum Pudding Competition
2. Purple
3. Accession Day
4. Your Servant
5. Commonwealth Games
6. Tree planting
7. Perpetua
8. Epsom Downs
9. Big Jubilee Lunch
10. Thank You Day
11. Life at Balmoral
12. Superbloom
13. Heinz
14. HM Sauce and Salad Queen
15. June the 2nd to June the 5th
16. 240
17. Over 1500
18. 8
19. False
20. Equestrian portrait of the Queen and Portrait of the Queen in 1952

ROYAL PROPERTIES

1. Windsor Castle
2. Balmoral Castle
3. Sandringham House
4. Holyrood Palace
5. Hillsborough Castle
6. 13
7. Hens
8. Malta
9. Clarence House
10. Little cottage
11. Tamarisk House
12. Frogmore Cottage
13. 6
14. Black truffles
15. 30 minutes
16. Balmoral Estate
17. Not subject to a bishop or archbishop
18. Queen Mary's dolls' house
19. Buckingham Palace

MISCELLANEOUS

1. 14
2. Margaret Thatcher
3. Dorgi
4. Arsenal
5. Australian
6. French
7. Whisper
8. Pigeons
9. Victoria
10. Tinned pineapple
11. Cocker Spaniel
12. James Bond
13. Brazil
14. Tony Blair
15. Gryffindor
16. Brooch
17. Tiara
18. Bagpipes
19. Poet Laureate
20. Rhino
21. Ration Coupons
22. Lyndon B. Johnson
23. Group Captain Peter Townsend
24. Sturgeon
25. Fell ponies
26. The Derby

27. Susan
28. Surveyor of the Queen's Pictures
29. Piper to the Sovereign
30. Partridge casserole
31. Oysters
32. Garlic
33. Smoked salmon, trout and mackerel
34. Special K
35. French
36. German
37. Cameroon and Rwanda
38. She was visiting in her role as Queen of Canada
39. Libya
40. Toilet paper
41. George II
42. Fruitcake
43. Chelmsford
44. Instagram

MATCH THE TITLE TO THE NAME

1. Prince Charles
2. Will and Kate
3. Prince Edward (Queen's son)
4. Prince Richard/Henry
5. Prince Edward (Queen's cousin)
6. Prince Andrew
7. Prince Philip
8. Prince Charles
9. David Armstrong-Jones
10. Wallis Simpson

LINE OF SUCCESSION

1. Prince Charles
2. Prince William
3. Prince George
4. Princess Charlotte
5. Prince Louis
6. Prince Harry
7. Archie Mountbatten-Windsor
8. Lilibet Diana Mountbatten-Windsor
9. Prince Andrew
10. Princess Beatrice
11. Princess Eugenie
12. August Philip Hawke Brooksbank
13. Prince Edward
14. James, Viscount Severn
15. Lady Louise Windsor
16. Anne, Princess Royal
17. Peter Phillips
18. Savannah Phillips
19. Isla Phillips
20. Zara Tindall

FERNHURST JUNIOR SCHOOL

Printed in Great Britain
by Amazon

82524290R00027